Who is Sam Harrington?

Written by Rick Osborne and K. Christie Bowler
Illustrated by Dara Goldman

Zonderkidz
The Children's Group of ZondervanPublishingHouse

The dreary little town of Coledale was not a fun place to live. No one showed up for the annual town picnic, most of the pews in the church were empty, and faces everywhere wore frowns. People passed each other without even saying hello. Old timers complained about the new folk, and the new folk complained about the old timers. But one day, everything changed.

Sunday morning, Jenny Pepper ran into Coledale Community Church, knocking Bobby Franks' glasses right off his face.

"Hey! Watch where you're going, clumsy!" he snarled. Jenny was already late. She glanced back, then raced into her class.

After the service, people complained as usual about the weather, the mayor, and the price of hamburgers. They even complained about Mr. Skritchen, the town grump, because he complained too much! Jenny ran down the aisle ahead of her parents. She put her back to the sanctuary's huge oak doors, braced her legs, and pushed them wide open. "Thank you, Jenny," her parents said, surprised.

Jenny grinned. "It's what Sam Harrington would do," she said.

"Sam who?" the Peppers asked. But Jenny had already run off toward their home just down the block.

On her way, Jenny noticed Bobby Franks trying to carry a wobbly stack of books almost as tall as he was. Then she saw Rocky, the school bully, riding around the corner toward Bobby. *That's what Bobby gets for yelling at me this morning,* she thought, watching to see what would happen. Suddenly she remembered Sam Harrington and called, "Look out!" Too late! Rocky's bike brushed against Bobby, and Bobby and his books tumbled to the ground.

As Jenny ran over, Bobby grumbled, "Leave me alone! I don't need your help."

"I'm sorry about knocking you down earlier," Jenny said. "I should've watched where I was going."

"Yeah," Bobby agreed, surprised. Then he added, "Aw, that's all right."

Jenny bent to help Bobby gather his books into two piles. "You sure read a lot!" she said. "That must be why you're so smart in school."

Bobby's cheeks went red as he ducked his head. Jenny helped him carry the books all the way to his house. When they arrived and the books were safe on the kitchen table, he said, "Uh, thanks, Jenny."

"No problem," Jenny replied. "That's what Sam Harrington would do." She waved and headed for home.

Later that afternoon, Bobby sat down under a tree and opened a book. But before he even started reading, he looked up and saw Lynda Snowdon crying as she walked toward him. "What now?" he muttered. Then he hollered, "What's the matter, Lynda?"

"I've lost my dog!" she sobbed.

Too bad, Bobby thought, turning back to his book. Then he remembered how good he had felt when Jenny had helped him. He closed his book and scrambled to his feet. "I'll help you find him." So off they went, calling, "Montrose! Mon-ty!"

Soon Bobby spotted a suspiciously woolly branch under a bush in Mr. Skritchen's yard. Bobby ran over to investigate. Sure enough, there was Monty, his leash all tangled up in the bush.

Mr. Skritchen yelled at them from his porch, waving his cane, "Get out of here. And stop that hollering!"

Lynda swallowed. "Yes, sir." She and Bobby quickly untangled Montrose, while the dog barked and licked Lynda's face all over.

"Thank you so much, Bobby," Lynda said.

Bobby waved as he ran home. "Aw, it's only what Sam Harrington would do."

Lynda skipped toward home with Montrose tugging on his leash beside her. By the school she saw Rocky Tanner kicking his bike, looking even meaner than usual. Lynda shivered and hurried past. After only a few steps, though, she turned back and asked, "Everything okay, Rocky?"

" 'Course not!" Rocky grunted, glaring at the bike. "I've got a flat tire, and I don't know how to fix it."

"Well . . .," Lynda began.

"Well, what?" Rocky demanded.

"Well, my dad helps me with my bike. I don't see why he couldn't fix yours if you want."

ocky stopped glaring at his bike and turned his frown on Lynda. "Really?" he asked suspiciously.

"Yeah. Really."

Rocky's frown became a smile. "Okay. That would be great!" He picked up his bike and walked it beside Lynda to her garage, where her father was working. Together, they fixed Rocky's tire, and he hopped on. "Thanks!" he called as he rode off. "I owe you!"

"Nope," Lynda answered. "We only did what Sam Harrington would do."

"Who's Sam Harrington?" Lynda's father asked. But Lynda was gone.

ocky whistled as he rode off to meet his buddies after school on Monday. As he rounded a corner, he slammed on his brakes and skidded to a stop. Right in front of him lay Coledale's junior soccer star, Sidney Thomas. He was rolling on the ground, groaning.

"What's up?" Rocky asked, looking at his watch and frowning. He was late.

"Ooh!" Sidney moaned. "It's my toe. I think I broke it!"

Rocky couldn't help grinning. The best soccer player in town out of commission because of a stubbed toe! *What a baby!* he thought, trying to hide his smile. He paused, thinking, then said, "Aw, relax. I'll help you home."

Rocky helped Sidney stand up and hop over to his bike. "Sit on the seat, and I'll push you," Rocky said.

"Thanks," Sidney said between whimpers.

"No sweat," Rocky answered.

Rocky balanced Sidney carefully on his bike and pushed him down the block toward Sidney's home.

"Ooohh!" wailed Sidney.

"Mrs. Thomas!" Rocky called as he got near Sidney's house. "Sidney's hurt." The Thomas's door flew open and Sidney's mom rushed out. "Oh dear," she said, helping Sidney off Rocky's bike and into the car. "You'll be all right," she told him, "but we'll head over to the clinic just to make sure it isn't broken. Thanks, Rocky."

"Yeah, thanks a lot," Sidney added.

Rocky climbed onto his bike, not sure what to say. He didn't get thanked very often. "Uh . . . that's what Sam Harrington would do," he said finally. And he rode away, whistling again, to meet his friends.

At the clinic, Sidney fixed a doll for a little girl named Tina. She hugged her doll and smiled at Sidney. "Wow!" she said. "You're so smart! Thanks."

Sidney smiled back. "You're welcome. After all, that's what Sam Harrington would do."

Tina went home and helped her brother find his baseball glove.
"That's what Sam Harrington would do," she said when he thanked her.

At the park, Tina's brother showed Florence, his team's newest player, how to hold the bat properly. And he threw perfect pitches to Ronnie, so Ronnie could practice batting. "That's what Sam Harrington would do," he explained.

Later, Florence took a batch of cookies to the sick Sorenson twins, saying, "That's what Sam Harrington would do."

Ronnie loaned his drum set to his neighbor Isaac. "Sam Harrington would," he said.

By Tuesday, those kids had found still more kids to be kind to, kids whose names they didn't even know. Soon children all over Coledale were doing nice things for one another, saying, "That's what Sam Harrington would do."

It happened in the library, the schoolyard, the swimming pool, and the park. It happened in the playground, the grocery store, the café, and the doughnut shop. It happened in streets and yards and ball fields—and even to Mr. Skritchen!

"Sam Harrington, eh?" Mr. Skritchen asked, as the grocer's son helped him carry heavy bags to his car. "I'd like to meet him."

Adults and parents watched and wondered about the changes coming over their town. Not even the old timers could remember so much kindness, so many smiling faces, and so many good deeds in Coledale!

And all over town, one name kept coming up: Sam Harrington. Everyone was asking the same question: "Who is Sam Harrington?" Children asked their parents. Teachers asked the principal. Workers asked their bosses. Old timers asked new folk, and new folk asked old timers. But no one—not even the children—knew the answer. And the man himself was nowhere to be found.

On Wednesday afternoon, Mr. Skritchen stopped complaining long enough to have an idea. "I've got it!" he yelled. "There's one person who knows every soul in Coledale."

"Of course!" Mrs. Snowdon exclaimed. "Pastor Lyle!"

Soon everyone was convinced that Pastor Lyle must surely know Sam Harrington. And the one place they were sure to find Pastor Lyle was at Coledale Community Church. The word spread quickly, and the whole town crowded into the church for the Wednesday evening service.

Every pew was packed with people squeezed in side by side. Children sat on parents' knees to make room for others. The aisles were full. The balcony was stacked to the rafters. And everywhere, as people jammed in, you could hear the whispers:

"Do you know who Sam Harrington is?"

"Any strangers here?"

"I heard Pastor Lyle is going to tell us."

"I hope Sam's here. I want to shake his hand."

At last, Pastor Lyle walked out of his study, closed the door, and approached the pulpit. The whispers died down and the crowd grew quiet. Every eye was fixed on the pastor.

The pastor put his hands on the sides of the pulpit and leaned forward. "Ladies and gentlemen, how wonderful to see our church filled to overflowing tonight! Before we begin, there is something we must clear up."

Here it comes, the people thought. *He's going to tell us!* They leaned forward eagerly.

Pastor Lyle took in a long breath and, in his best preaching voice, asked, "Who is Sam Harrington?"

The whole church sighed in disappointment. Pastor Lyle didn't know. "Does anyone know who Sam Harrington is?" he asked again.

Silence. Then a small voice piped up. "I know who he is. Don't you?"

Every head turned toward Jenny Pepper. "Miss James told us," she said.

Every eye turned to Miss James, the Sunday school teacher. Her jaw dropped, for she'd been asking the same question as everyone else! She shrugged and held up her empty hands. "I'm sorry, Jenny," she said. "But I don't think I've heard of Sam Harrington."

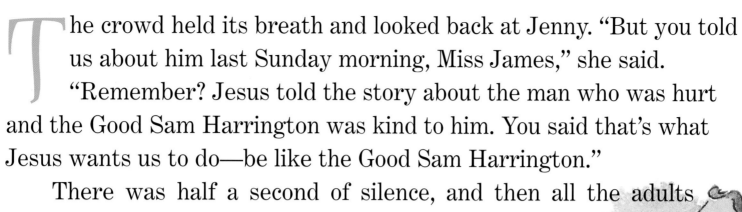

The crowd held its breath and looked back at Jenny. "But you told us about him last Sunday morning, Miss James," she said.

"Remember? Jesus told the story about the man who was hurt and the Good Sam Harrington was kind to him. You said that's what Jesus wants us to do—be like the Good Sam Harrington."

There was half a second of silence, and then all the adults began to laugh! Jenny was more puzzled than ever.

Pastor Lyle asked Jenny to come to the front. He lifted her onto the the pulpit. "Citizens of Coledale," he said in his wonderful, rich preaching voice, "Jenny is absolutely right! Jesus wants us to be like Sam Harrington. When Sam found a man hurt on the road, he didn't walk by as others had. No, the Good Sam Harrington wrapped the man's wounds and put him on his donkey. Then he took him to an inn where he could get better. Sam's kindness saved that man's life."

Pastor Lyle paused and smiled at Jenny. "And over the past few days," he said, "we have seen the power of kindness! It changes hearts and people and even towns! Three cheers for Jenny and Sam Harrington!"

"Hip-hip-hooray!"

"Hip-hip-hooray!"

"HIP-HIP-HOORAY!"

That day the townspeople decided they'd be a friendly, kind town where good deeds happen every day. And Coledale has never been the same! Now as you drive into Coledale, you'll see that the population has grown by one.

The Good Samaritan

(Luke 10:25, 29-37)

One day an authority on the law stood up to put Jesus to the test. . . . So he asked Jesus, "And who is my neighbor?"

Jesus replied, "A man was going down from Jerusalem to Jericho. Robbers attacked him. They stripped off his clothes and beat him. Then they went away, leaving him almost dead. A priest happened to be going down that same road. When he saw the man, he passed by on the other side. A Levite also came by. When he saw the man, he passed by on the other side too.

"But a Samaritan came to the place where the man was. When he saw the man, he felt sorry for him. He went to him, poured olive oil and wine on his wounds and bandaged them. Then he put the man on his own donkey. He took him to an inn and took care of him. The next day he took out two silver coins. He gave them to the owner of the inn. 'Take care of him,' he said. 'When I return, I will pay you back for any extra expense you may have.'

"Which of the three do you think was a neighbor to the man who was attacked by robbers?"

The authority on the law replied, "The one who felt sorry for him."

Jesus told him, "Go and do as he did."

Who Is Sam Harrington?
Copyright © 2000 by Lightwave Publishing, Inc.
Requests for information should be addressed to:

Zonder**kidz**

The Children's Group of ZondervanPublishingHouse
Grand Rapids, Michigan 49530
www.zonderkidz.com

Interior design by Lisa Workman
Printed in China
00 01 02 03 04 05 /v HK/ 10 9 8 7 6 5 4 3 2 1